Stepping Stones

Stepping Stones

A collection of poems by

Chad A. Armel

GREENSBORO, NORTH CAROLINA, USA

ISBN 978-0-6151-4315-6

Printed in the United States of America.

To my parents, who have done the best that they can do to raise a decent young man. I say thanks for all that you have sacrificed. To my wonderful wife, whom I owe my life to; for being there through thick and thin, and never walking away. You are my true inspiration. I thank you for always being behind my every idea and dream. I also thank you for blessing me with a wonderful child. To my son, for showing me what true unconditional love is really all about. A fathers love for a child is something I never could have imagined. To my two lovely sisters and their families. Thank you for bringing joy into everyone's lives. To my grandparents and all those who have helped me get to where I am today. May all the ones we lost truly rest in peace. To Pastor Paul, and our current pastor, Pastor Don. To all my church family, both previous and current. I sincerely give you thanks, and may God bless each and every one of you.

Contents

Contents

"Stepping Stones"

Events are only stepping stones in life.
One event followed by another, then by another.
Falling just below our feet, to keep us moving ahead.
Some events may seem broken,
Just as a stepping stone,
That has had many feet pass along it.
These events may not be as we planned,
But circumstance will sometimes,
Beat us to the stepping stone, leaving us stumbling,
While we try to not step on the crack.
In the end, when we look back,
We will find that each event, just as each stepping stone,
Gathers together to make a path.
This path, is the path of our lives.
The only thing we have control over,
Is which stone we choose to step on.
It is these decisions that create the events of the next step.

"True Love"

My dear,
You have shown me,
The greatest love I've ever known.

A love,
That I completely failed to see.

A love,
Not of material things.

A love,
Not of any one woman here on earth.

A love,
Overseen by so many.

This love I speak of,
Is that of myself.

"Angel Eyes"

The roses smelled of sunny days,
The air of summer fun.

As she began to laugh and play,
The day has just begun.

Innocent and full of grace,
The world sits by and waits.

Too young to know what lies beyond,
The love and all the hate.

The world is perfect,
When you view it,
Through her angel eyes.

If only she could keep that view,
As time and years pass by.

"The Truth I Long For"

Lord, grant me peace and happiness,
Not of the world around me,
But of myself.

Content in what life presents to me,
Whether it be,
That of poor or that of wealth.

As I meditate on your word,
May you speak to me,
The truth I long for.

And may I never fill my heart
With greed which keeps me
Wanting more.

Amen

"Time"

Time keeps ticking,

Second by second, minute by minute,
Hour by hour,
Time keeps ticking.

Day by day, month by month,
Year by year,
Time keeps ticking.

When I sleep,
Time keeps ticking.

When I wake,
Time keeps ticking.

If I wait for an opportunity,
Or I make opportunity,
Either way,
Time keeps ticking.

"The Only Way"

When I look into my heart I find,
I can't control it all.

When I look into my soul I find,
At times I have to fall.

When I look into this world I find,
More troubles every day.

When I look into God's word I find,
It is the only way.

"Simply I Love You"

Simply, I Love You.

There are no other words
To describe the feelings
I have for you.

There is no other way
To show you my Love is true.

No feeling has ever been
This strong, this sincere.

My truest happiness,
Only comes when you are near.

For this I say,
Simply,
I LOVE YOU.

"One Must"

To understand life,
One must understand his word.

To understand his word,
One must be willing to accept.

To be willing to accept,
One must be in search of the truth.

To be in search of the truth,
One must ask.

"Come Home My Son"

The old man was dying,
Close to his last breath.

How could it be,
A man so loving,
Could die a lonely death.

His wife is gone,
She passed away,
So many years ago.

He lives each day,
Missing his kids,
But they seem to never show.

He prays to God,
And asks the Lord,
Is this how it's going to end?

The Lord says,
Come home my son,
You'll never be lonely again.

"As The Raindrops Fall"

The calmness of the raindrops,
Quiets my mind and soul.

Helps me think of better ways,
To accomplish all my goals.

And as I speak of goals,
I think,
What are they anyway?

Do we ever stick to them,
Or forget them in a day?

What is it that I'm meant to be,
Do I have a call?

All these thoughts , just pass by,
As the raindrops fall.

"Another World"

She is a gift from God,
So innocent and sweet.

She looks just like her mother,
From her head down to her feet.

It's amazing how she grew so fast,
And now leaving the nest.

He knows he's not the perfect dad,
But he's done his best.

As she drives away, a tear,
Falls from his cheek to the ground.

Daddy's little girl now has,
Another world to be found.

"When I'm At the Gates"

Dear lord, give me the strength,
To believe in all I do.

Help me build my faith,
And in my veins, your love flow through.

Help me be the very best,
Man that I can be.

Guide me to marry the one I love,
And raise a family.

Show me what the meaning,
Of my life is meant to be.

So when I'm at the gates My Lord,
You will accept me.

"One"

My love for you has grown through the years.
From a love that only existed for a new found friend,
To that of my true love, that cannot be described in words.
Only myself and the Lord truly know,
How much love flows through my veins for you.
In the event that you were to walk away,
My life would be in pieces,
Leaving me with only memories,
Of the most perfect love.
That love in which a man could only dream of,
Is the love that we share in these very days.
Hanging from Heaven's gates,
To guide us through the events of life.
Together we walk, and together we fall,
But still we continue on the same path.
Hand in hand, stepping together,
We follow each other's footsteps.
Sharing each other's dreams and desires.
Continuing to learn each other more each day,
All the while, growing as one.

"Look At Your Soul"

Look at that man and laugh,
That is what your mind tells you to do,
When you see the homeless man on the street.

Look at that woman and criticize her weight,
That is what your mind tells you to do,
When you see the lady eating at the restaurant.

Look at the other woman,
And obsess over her gorgeous body,
That is what your mind tells you to do,
As she passes by.

Look at your spouse in disgust and yell at her,
That is what your mind tells you to do,
When she does something that you oppose.

Look at your soul in need for true answers,
That is what your heart tells you to do,
When you face the problems of this world.

"With A Loving Hand"

The fields are green, the sky is blue,
The sun is shining bright.

That's how I feel, when I look at you,
Every day and night.

All my troubles, and all my worries,
Leave my soul and mind.

When I look into your eyes,
It's all just left behind.

A blessing from the Heavens,
An Angel in my life.

The kind of girl that any man,
Would love to make his wife.

Never disrespect you,
And do all that I can.

To honor and protect you,
With a loving hand.

"Love Is True"

Life is only,
But what you make it.

Love is true,
But never forsake it.

Never mistake it,
For wants or needs.

Once your heart breaks,
It eternally bleeds.

"Each Day"

Each day is like a canvas,
Fresh, dry, and clear.

Waiting for a painting,
Of happiness or tears.

Decisions are like brushes,
Each thought is like a stroke.

At the end of your day,
Your painting is what you spoke.

"God's Joining"

I thank him for unanswered prayers,
I thank him for hard times,
I thank him for leading me in directions,
I thought were wrong.
Because at the end of the trail,
I met you, and from then
we continued down another trail together.
Full of happiness and love,
Sun shining,
Birds chirping.
It is the trail of true life.
And God is with us,
Smiling at his wonderful joining.
It is truly a wonderful thing.

"Through My Window"

Through my window,
I can see the sun shining bright.

Through my window,
I can see the stars shining at night.

Through my window,
I can see the birds flying through the sky.

Through my window,
I can see the neighbors passing by.

Through my window,
I can see all women, and all men.

Through my window,
I can see the work of my Lord again.

"In My Sleep"

Talking in my sleep,
I wake up crying.
My relationship has just ended.
I have done nothing wrong.
Nothing that shall lead to this.
Soothing are the tears,
That fall down my cheek.
At the same time,
Causing pain.
I wipe the tears,
Each time adding more tears,
More pain,
More sorrow.
It's too much to handle.
My mind races.
Suddenly I realize,
It was only a dream.
Not a dream,
But a nightmare.

"The Lord Said"

I was lost, but the Lord said,
You shall be found.

I was weak, but the Lord said,
You shall stand on solid ground.

I was afraid, but the Lord said,
You shall not fear.

I was lonely, but the Lord said,
Your father is near.

I was ignorant, but the Lord said,
You shall find wisdom and might.

I could not see, but the Lord said,
You shall see the light.

"When I Ask You"

When I ask you to Love me,
I don't mean half-heartedly.

When I ask you to Love me,
I don't mean with conditions.

When I ask you to Love me,
I don't mean for less than a lifetime.

For I Love You,
Whole-heartedly, unconditionally,
And for Eternity.

"A Beautiful Day"

Though the day is cloudy,
The sun still shines bright.
Bright as the most lovely day,
On a flower filled spring afternoon,
With birds singing,
And the breeze gathering future rose buds.
Petals of a wonderful beauty,
Rest upon the greenest grass.
Skies of blue are at their peak,
Glistening with a color tone,
As crisp as a perfect picture.
An aroma as fresh as the purest air,
Calmly and softly rests upon your nose.
With a feeling of complete peace,
You gather your thoughts in total amazement.
For the day is cloudy.
But with the Lord in your heart,
It is the most beautiful day,
That you have ever witnessed,
In all your years.

"Your Voice"

My Love,
I miss you deeply.
So deep it hurts.
In fact,
I feel pain in my heart,
Longing for you,
As if we have not talked in months.
For one day is equal to an eternity,
Without the tone
Of your lovely voice in my ear.
It is a voice of Heavenly value,
Of Love,
Of truth,
Of pure and honest compassion.
This is what I feel,
When we speak.
And this is what I wish
To take with me,
When my time is through.
The longing for your most
Wonderful voice to be heard.
Because of you I know,
that when that time has come,
we will one day join again,
and the Lord will grant my heart
With what it longs for.

"All That She Has"

Lying here with you by my side,
Makes me feel complete.
What is it,
That makes a man feel this secure.
The warmth that comes from,
The heart of a woman like you.
Could keep such a man warm,
Through the coldest winter days.
Thus, producing even more warmth,
By taming the heart of the man.
What a woman,
A great woman in deed.
To have such compassion,
To share unconditionally,
And without thought.
With no needs or desires,
But to give all that she has,
For this man.
This is Love,
True Love.

"Freedom Prayer"

My fellow people of this great land,
Shall we never to forget those,
That have perished with honor,
For the freedom that we live with.
Unto thy Lord, I do pray,
That he bless their loved one's souls.

This poem is dedicated to those who have fought, died, and served to give me the freedoms that I enjoy today. May God Bless you all. Thank you!

"Soothing Waves"

There's something about the waters,
Crisp clean sound.
Each wave like an individual,
With it's own personality.
Each sound, in it's own soothing way,
Adding to the delight of calmness and peace.
Though it is nothing like an ocean wave,
The orchestra of waves that is produced,
By this small body of water,
Is much to my delight a peaceful presence,
Among the stressful and nonstop world,
In which we live in today.
In it's own way, it is like a vacation,
In my back yard.
Each time, producing new memories,
And a new sense of peace.
A renewed hope,
That there are more places similar to this,
That we can escape to,
And release our worries and fears.

"In The End"

I broke her heart,
Left her alone.
She didn't know,
Which way to turn.
So many times,
She said she cared.
But in the end,
I wasn't there.
All this time,
I loved her so,
But in the end,
She didn't know.

"Bridges Are Burned"

You see a man on the street,
Begging for some change.
You think he looks weird,
You think he looks strange.
You start to shy away,
Walk to the other side.
The next day you see him,
So you try to hide.
Never thinking about,
What's really going on.
You go home to your kids,
But he has no home.
You go on with your life,
But that's his life.
He's alone through the night,
Wishing for some light.
A blessing from God,
Is what he prays
You could have been the blessing,
But you walked away.
All he needed was a dime;
One minute of your time.
You could have changed his life,
With one minute and a line.
You chose the other route,
Thinking no-one would care.
But God's looking down,
And he knows you were there.
So what's it going to be,
If the table is turned.
And you need a helping hand,
But the bridges are burned.

Thinking back reminiscing,
About when you were a kid.
And all of the terrible,
Things that you did.
Little Bobby was slower,
Then the average kid.
So they put him in a class,
On a lower grid.
Every time you would see him,
He was walking alone.
Every time he would whisper,
He was talking alone.
Everybody would laugh,
And call him a freak.
But in God's eyes,
He was just unique.
A little bit slower,
And a little bit shy.
But if you stopped to get to know him,
He is a regular guy.
He has a big heart,
But nobody knows.
Because all they see of him,
Is what the outside shows.
A little boy that's always,
Talking to himself.
But he's really talking to God,
Asking for some help.
So what's it going to be,
If the table is turned.
And you need a helping hand,
But the bridges are burned.

"Find Your Way"

Never give up,
Never give in.
Never look back,
To where you've been.
Never look forward,
Until you examine today.
Because now is the time,
To find your way.

"Is Love"

They say love is blind,
But is this so?
If one is in love,
How does one know?
Is it feelings,
Or deeper still?
Is love an emotion,
Is that for real?
Is love in the heart,
Or is love in the soul?
Is love overlooked,
By only a fool?
Is love only lust,
Or can it be true.
It's all in yourself,
It's all up to you.

"The God unto We Pray"

Planes falling out of the sky,
We don't know why.
People going out of control,
Living in lies.
Young soldiers fighting for freedom,
Why do they die?
Leaving yet another,
Heartbroken mother to cry.
Another hero to lay rest,
As we say our goodbye.
Why can't we live as one,
And place our Lord up high?
Our religions remain different,
But there's truly one God.
Looking down on all of us,
Will he give a nod?
At the actions that we take;
The decisions that we make.
For when we stand up at the gates,
There's no room for mistakes.
Our very soul relies on,
What we make of every day.
So stop and think about the God,
Which unto we pray.

"It's A New Day"

I ask you not to make up for lost time.
I would never ask of such a thing.
I ask you not to change the things in the past,
For the time has passed and the day's are new.
The decisions that we make,
Carve our paths through life.
And not everyone will agree,
On the path that we take.
But in the end,
Our paths will all meet again.
And our hearts will be judged,
Not our paths.
For no-one is perfect,
And we shall not judge.
I ask you only,
To make the best of your days.
And never forget,
Where your heart lies.
Together we can make the best,
Of our days that we have left.
For you are still my dad,
And I am still your son.
Though we don't see each other often,
You are still thought of.
And the memories I have,
From my younger days,
Are no less that I could ask for.
Let's not live through memories,
But build new ones.
Living for the future,
Not for the past.
It's a new day,
Let's make the best of it.

"To Waste the Mind"

The mind is a terrible thing to waste;
Who has actually contemplated,
On what it really means,
To have wasted ones mind?
For those who have not exceeded
Beyond ones comfort zone,
There are parts of the mind,
That have wasted over time.
But for some, it is more;
For intellectual pleasures,
And meaningless engagements
Of social interaction,
The mind has been wasted.
Increasing the chances of the mind,
Never once again being as sharp,
As it's original potential.
The sheer ignorance for once self,
And one's well being,
Has left the mind unchallenged intellectually,
But challenged in a physical sense.
Never again to exceed,
To new levels.

"Questions That I Ask"

Is it freedom
Is it oil
Is it enemy
Is it God
Is it right
Is it wrong
Is it land
Is it not
Is it leader
Is it world
Is it country
Is it man
Is it war
Is it conflict
Is it small
Is it grand

"In The Blink of An Eye"

In the blink of an eye,
Our world had changed.
Not the world of one single nation,
But the world of many nations.
The innocent were affected,
And lives were lost.
Only to affect more innocent in return,
Only to lose more lives.
What is it that brings hate,
Into a world of nations?
Greed?
Lust?
Power?
Money?
More importantly,
What can bring peace to this Great Land,
And to the lands that surround us?
This is the question,
We must all think about.
For our time is short,
And what do we have to leave?

"True Beauty"

Beauty must lye,
In the eye of the beholder.

A moment to cry,
Must lye in a shoulder.

But only of one,
Who is loving to all.

And will reach out,
To lift up somebody who falls.

For inside your heart,
True beauty will grow.

And through others eyes,
True beauty will show.

"As The Tide Comes In"

As the tide comes in,
It seems to have a way,
Of washing all worries,
Cleansing the soul,
And renewing the mind.
Creating a fresh start,
For ones very existence.
As the tide comes in,
Each wave represents,
A new spirit that,
Fills the soul with joy.
Allowing ones perspective,
On life to be optimistic,
Full of enthusiasm,
And eagerness to achieve,
The most out of one's life.

"Window of Opportunity"

A window of opportunity,
May appear to be small.
But if the opportunity is grabbed,
The window can be opened.
That small window can be overlooked,
Or can be noticed for it's potential,
To be a life changing event.
It is through the eyes of a certain few,
That window will become a door to success.

"I Cannot Live Without"

Though it may seem like I have walked away,
Lord I promise you I have not.
Man is not perfect, and I am,
A perfect example of that.
If I lived a life of no sin,
Then I would need no help.
But because I cannot live such a life,
I ask for your help.
Through you, I now know that,
I cannot be perfect,
And I can live with that.
The one thing that I found,
I cannot live without,
Is you Lord.

"My Son"

I look into your eyes My Son.
I could never have imagined the joy you bring,
Into my life, my heart, and my soul.
The day you were born, I was reborn as well.
I grew from a young man to a father in that moment.
That special moment in life when you took your first breath,
We took that breath together.
From that day on, the meaning of life has changed,
Because the meaning of life is no longer about me,
But it is about you. For the truth is, my life is your life,
And I would die for you My Son.
You are too young to truly understand this truth,
But one day soon, you will know the depth of my love.
I will never let you go into the world empty handed,
But I will give you the tools to survive.
I will never let you go out into this world alone,
For I will be by your side.
I will be here for you until my final days,
For you are my blood, and you are My Son